MINITEN

RULES OF THE GAME

Illustrations by Colin Gordon

I0365979

The Rules of Miniten as adopted by
the Amateur Miniten Association of Great Britain

© Amateur Miniten Association

Illustrations by Colin Gordon

The information in this book is true and complete to
the best of the Publisher's knowledge. The Publisher
wishes to thank those who have greatly assisted in this
publication. Every effort has been made to ensure that
credits accurately comply with information supplied.
They deeply regret if despite their concerted efforts,
if any copyright owners have been unintentionally
overlooked or omitted. The Publisher will amend any
such errors in any future edition if they are brought to
The Publisher's attention.

A CIP catalogue record of this book is available from
The British Library.

MINITEN

RULES OF THE GAME

Illustrations by Colin Gordon

WOLFBAIT
UNDER THE COUNTER CULTURE

Contents

Introduction 7

Rules of the Game 8

The Singles Game 12

The Double Game 18

The Tie Break 20

Appendixes

   Rules for Regional Championship Playoffs 22

   Rules for the National Doubles Finals 24

   Rules for Junior events 25

   Rules of Eligibility 26

Introduction

MINITEN is a portmanteau word, derived from mini and tennis. The game was created by naturists in the 1930s and was taken up over time by various sporting and outdoor organisations.

Mr R. Douglas Ogden, a Manchester-based businessman with an interest in sporting activities drew up the original rules. Players, however, soon realised the limitations which these rules imposed on the game, especially the pace. This resulted in the game evolving towards a lower net and a longer service court, to facilitate a faster and infinitely more exciting game. It also made it easier for the beginner in terms of clearing the net and grounding the ball within the confines of the court.

In 1966 a group of enthusiasts in the South of England set out to formalise the rules of play. This resulted in The Amateur Miniten Association of Great Britain being formed.

The rules and scoring are similar to lawn tennis, and standard tennis balls are used. The court is much smaller, and instead of racquets, players use wooden bats known as thugs, which are shaped like a box around the player's hand

The popularity of miniten has ebbed and waned over the years. The Amateur Miniten Association seems to be inactive in any meaningful way at present. I do hope that in publishing this booklet I manage to contribute in some way to a renewed interest in the sport.

Rules of the Game

As adopted by the Amateur Miniten Association of Great Britain.

1. The COURT shall be rectangular in shape and 13715mm (45ft) in length for both Singles and Doubles play. The Doubles court shall be 6400mm (21ft) in width, and the Singles court shall be 5500mm (18ft) in width.

   The Service Court shall be marked by a Rear Service Line 1375mm (4.5ft) from the Baseline. The Rear Service Line shall only extend across the Singles Court and shall be 5500mm (18ft) long. From the centre of the net, a line parallel to the Sidelines shall extend to the centre of the Rear Service Line and a Centre Mark shall project 150mm (6in) inwards from the Baseline.

2. The NET shall be continuous from top to ground and from post to post. The net shall be 990mm (3.25ft) in height at the Doubles Sidelines and 915mm in height at the centre of the court. The net shall be suspended from a cord, wire or cable and shall have a white band about 51mm – 63mm (2 – 2.5in) deep at the point from which the net is suspended.

THE COURT

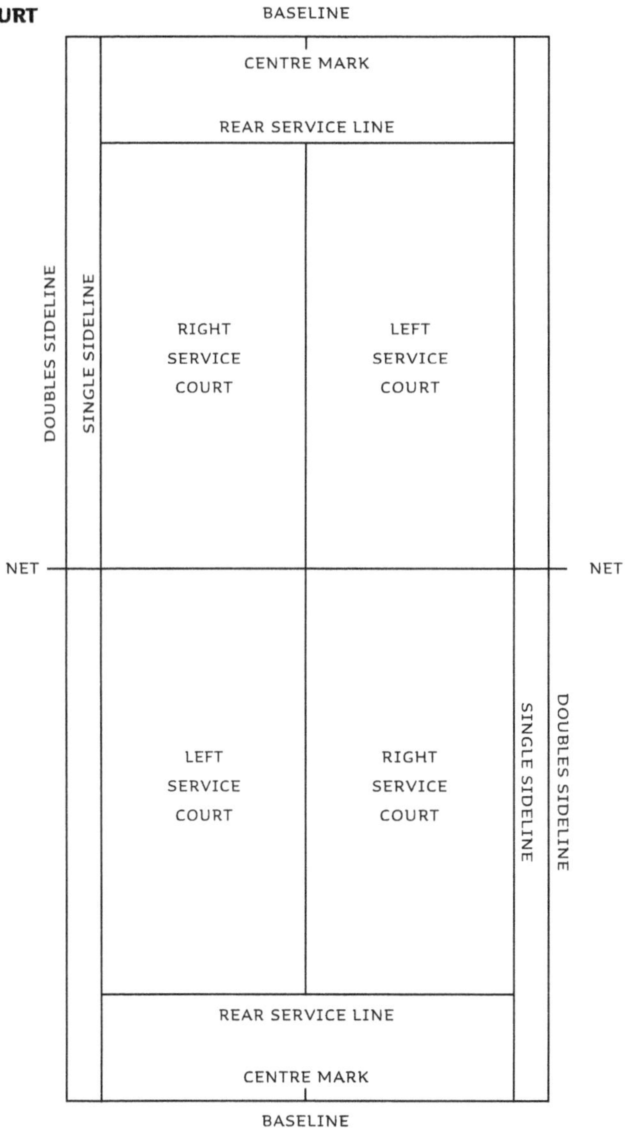

BASELINE
CENTRE MARK
REAR SERVICE LINE
DOUBLES SIDELINE
SINGLE SIDELINE
RIGHT SERVICE COURT
LEFT SERVICE COURT
NET
NET
LEFT SERVICE COURT
RIGHT SERVICE COURT
SINGLE SIDELINE
DOUBLES SIDELINE
REAR SERVICE LINE
CENTRE MARK
BASELINE

3.a The THUG shall be the term used to describe the double-faced bat with which the game is played. The faces shall be constructed of wood and shall not exceed 270mm (10.5in). A handle shall be set internally to the faces, and the faces shall be left uncovered by any substance other than a preservative of stain, paint, varnish, or other like fluid. Nothing shall project beyond the faces.

3.b The BALL shall be of an LTA (Lawn Tennis Association) approved standard.

TYPICAL TYPES OF THUGS

SQUARE

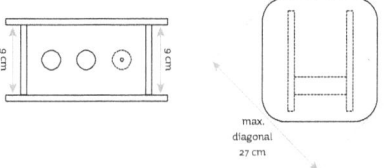
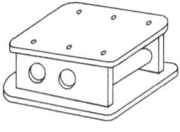

max. diagonal 27 cm

OBLONG

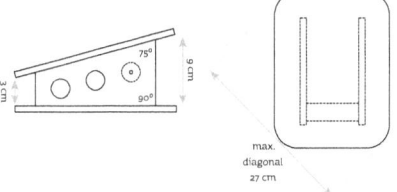
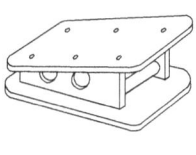

max. diagonal 27 cm

ROUND

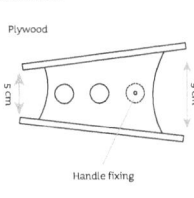
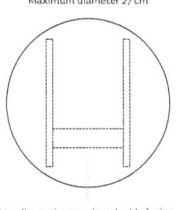
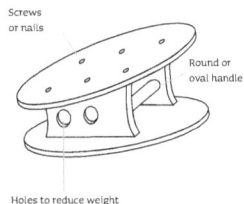

Plywood

Handle fixing

Maximum diameter 27 cm

Handle can be anywhere inside facings

Screws or nails

Round or oval handle

Holes to reduce weight

TENNIS GRIP

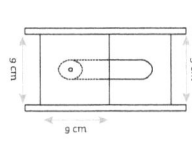
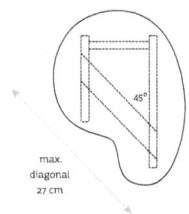
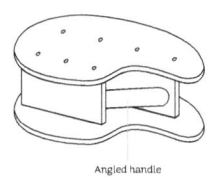

max. diagonal 27 cm

Angled handle

THE SINGLES GAME

4. The PLAYERS shall stand on opposite sides of the net; the one who first delivers the ball shall be termed the Server, the other the Receiver.

5. The CHOICE of sides and the right to be Server or Receiver in the first game shall be decided by a toss. If the winner of the toss elects to be Server or Receiver his opponent shall have the choice of sides. If the winner of the toss elects to have the choice of sides his opponent shall have the choice to be Server or Receiver. The winner of the toss may, if he so chooses, require his opponent to make first choice.

6. The SERVICE shall be delivered in the following manner – the feet shall be behind the Baseline and between the Service Line and the Singles Court Sideline. Contact with the ground behind the Baseline with both feet or one foot must be continuous from the start of the service: it is permissible, however, to have one foot over the Baseline, but not touching the ground, when the ball is struck. The service shall be from behind the right and left courts alternately, beginning with the right in every game.

The server shall project the ball by hand into the air in any direction strike it with his thug before it touches the ground. The Delivery shall be deemed to have been completed at the moment of contact between the Thug and the Ball. The ball shall then pass directly over the net and hit the ground within the diagonally opposite Service Court, or upon any line surrounding such court, before the Receiver returns it.

The service is a fault if the Server commits any breach of the above rule, but if the ball strikes a natural hazard or hit the top of the net and continue in flight so as to drop within the diagonally opposite Service Court, a let shall be called, and the service played again without change to the score.

After a fault (if it be the first fault) the Server shall serve again from behind the same half of the court from which he served that fault. If the second service is a fault, the point is lost to the Server, the players shall change to the positions for the playing of the next point to be played and the score shall be called. It shall be an understood fact that the calling of the score signals readiness to commence the next point unless either player shall, before the next service is delivered, signify that he is not ready to commence play. A fault may not be claimed after the next service has been delivered. If a Receiver attempts to make a return from a service he shall have deemed to have been ready to receive and the point shall be a good one.

7. ORDER OF PLAY. The game shall be played as shown in Rule 6. At the end of the first game, the Receiver shall become the Server and vice versa, and so on, alternately in all the subsequent games of a match. If a player serve out of turn, the player who ought to have served shall serve as soon as the mistake is discovered, but all points scored before the mistake be discovered shall count. If a game shall have been completed before such discovery, the order of service remains as altered. A fault served before such discovery shall not be reckoned. The players shall change sides after each first, third and subsequent odd game of each set, and at the end of each set.

8. The BALL is in play from the moment at which it is delivered in service (unless a fault or a let) and remains in play until the point is decided.

9. The SERVER wins the point if the ball touches the Receiver or anything which he wears or carries before the ball strikes the ground or if the Receiver otherwise loses a point as provided by Rule 11.

10. The RECEIVER wins the point if the Server loses the point as provided by Rule 11.

11. The player loses the point if:

   a) he fails, before the ball in play has hit the ground twice consecutively, to return it directly over the net (except as provided in Rule 15) or

   b) he returns the ball in play so that it hits the ground, a permanent fixture, or other object, outside any of the lines which bound his opponent's court or

   c) he volleys the ball and fails to make a good return even when standing outside the court or

   d) he touches or strikes the ball in play with his Thug more than once in making a stroke or

   e) he or his Thug (in his hand or otherwise) or anything which he wears or carries, touches the net, posts, cord or metal cable, or band, or the ground within his opponent's court at any time while the ball is in play or

f) he volleys the ball before it has passed the net or

g) the ball in play touches anything which he wears or carries, except his Thug, in his hands or hand or

h) he throws his Thug at and hits the ball

i) he drops anything which he carries (except his Thug) while the ball is in play.

12. A BALL falling on a line shall be deemed as falling in the court bounded by that line.

13. If the BALL in play touches a permanent fixture (except as provided in Rule 14a in respect of court fittings), a let shall be called and the point played again without change to the score as it stood at the start of the point. Overhanging branches and the like shall come within this category, but not the boundary fencing.

14. It is a GOOD RETURN if:

    a) the ball touches the net, posts, cord or metal cable or band, provided that it passes over any of them and hits the ground within the court

    b) the ball be returned outside the posts, either above or below the level of the net band, even tough it touches the post, provided that it hits the ground within the proper court.

c) the player's Thug pass the net, either over or round, after he has returned the ball provided the ball passes the net before being played and be properly returned.

15. In CASE a player is hindered making a stroke by anything not within his control, the point shall be termed a 'let' and replayed.

16. If a PLAYER wins the first point, the score is called 15 for that player; on winning his second point the score is called 30 for that player; on winning his third point the score is called 40 for that player, and the fourth point won by a player is scored game for that player except as below:

- If both players have scored three points, the score is called deuce; at which the next point scored by the player is called advantage for that player. If the same player wins the next point he wins the game; if the other player wins the next point, however, the score is called deuce.

- The player who wins two consecutive points immediately following the score at deuce wins the game.

17. The SET shall be won by the first player to win six games, except that if the score reaches 5 games all, the set be not completed until one player is two games in front.

The tie-break will come into operation when the score is 6 games all, in all sets except the last, when a normal full set will be played (See Rule 27).

18. The MAXIMUM number of sets in an official match shall be 5, but there shall be a maximum of three sets where women take part.

19. EXCEPT where otherwise stated, every reference in these rules to the masculine includes the feminine gender.

THE DOUBLES GAME

20. The PREVIOUS rules shall apply to the Doubles Game, except as below:

21. The PAIR who have the right to serve in the first game of each set may decide which partner may do so, and the opposing pair may decide similarly for the second game. The partner of the player who served in the first game shall serve in the third game, the partner of the player who served in the second game shall serve in the fourth game, and so on in the same order in all subsequent games of a set.

22. The ORDER OF SERVICE having been arranged may not be altered during the set, but it may be changed at the beginning of each new set. Similarly, the order of receiving services may not be changed before the end of a set, but they may be so at the beginning of a new set.

23. The SERVICE is a fault as provided in Rule 6, or if the ball served touches the Server's partner or anything which he wears or carries; but if the ball served touches the partner of the Receiver or anything which he wears or carries, before it hits the ground, the Server wins the point.

24. If a PARTNER serves out of his turn, the partner who ought to have served shall serve as soon as the mistake is discovered, but all points scored, and any fault served before such discovery, shall be reckoned. If a game shall have been completed before such discovery, the order of service remains as altered.

25. The PLAYERS to receive the service shall receive alternately throughout each game. The order thus established shall not be altered during the set.

26. The BALL shall be struck alternately by either player of the opposing pairs, and if a player touches the ball in play with his Thug in contravention of this rule, his opponents win the point.

THE TIE-BREAK

27. The tie-break will come into operation when the score is 6-6 in all sets except the last, when a normal full set will be played.

SINGLES

a) Players do not change ends at the start of the tie-break.

b) Service order shall be continuous and the player whose turn it is to serve shall be the Server for the first point. His or her opponent shall then be the Server for the next two points and then each player shall serve alternately, two points at a time, until the winner of the tie-break and set has been decided.

c) At the start of the tie-break the initial service shall be from the left-hand court. Thereafter each service shall be delivered alternately from the right-hand court and the left-hand court, beginning with the right-hand court.

d) A player who wins 9 points and leads by at least 2 points shall win the tie-break and the set. If the score reaches 8 points all the tie-break shall continue until a two-point lead has been gained.

e) Players shall change ends after every six points have been played and at the conclusion of the tie-break, irrespective of the number of points played.

f) The player who served first in the tie-break shall receive service in the first game of the following set.

DOUBLES

a) The procedure for the Singles game shall apply to the Doubles game also.

b) The serving order of the Doubles game shall follow the same order as previously in that set until the winners on the tie-break have been decided.

c) The pair serving first in the tie-break shall receive service in the first game of the following set.

Appendixes

Rules for Regional Championship Playoffs

1. The Regional Championships will be decided on a knockout basis.

2. The Championship games will be the best of three sets with a tie-break at six all in each set.

3. Seeding will be at the discretion of the Tournament Organiser.

4. Two pairs in each event may be seeded. One to go to the top of the draw and one to go to the bottom.

5. The Championship finalists will qualify for the National Doubles Final. Competitors who elect to take part in the Regional Championships only must notify the Tournament Organiser at the end of the tournament.

6. The remaining two qualifying places will be decided upon a league basis.

7. Results of games which have taken place in the knockout event will be transferred to the league.

8. In all qualifying games one point will be awarded for a win.

9. The duration of matches in the league is at the discretion of the Tournament Organiser, but will normally be decided by the best of three sets with a tie-break at six all in each set.

10. The league will be split into two halves, all losers in each half of the knockout draw will play each other. The top two teams in each half will play in the following way:

    Top half of the draw bottom half of the draw
    1 v 2   2 v 1

The top two teams will qualify as 3 and 4.

11. In the event of a tie on points, the games difference from league and knockout games will be taken into account. If the league is being played to one set then the games difference from the knockout will be taken from the final set.

12. The AMinA (The Amateur Miniten Association) rules will apply in all cases.

13. If any of the qualifiers decide not to play in the National Doubles Finals they must notify the AMinA Secretary, not less than fourteen days prior to the National Finals. The Secretary will then offer a qualifying place in the Finals to the team with the next highest score.

14. The Tournament Organiser is to notify the AMinA Secretary of the results in each event.

15. Only *bona fide* members of clubs affiliated to the Amateur Miniten Association may enter the competition.

Rules for the National Doubles Finals

1. The Championship games will be the best of three sets with a tie-break in each set. The Mixed and Ladies' Finals will be the best of three sets; there will be no tie-break in the final set. The Men's Final will be the best of five sets; there will be no tie-break in the final set.

2. AMinA rules will apply in all cases.

3. There will be a Plate Tournament for the first round losers. The format for the Plate Tournament will be at the discretion of the Tournament Organiser, but will normally be the best of three sets.

4. Losing semi-finalists may play for third place, at the discretion of the Tournament organiser.

5. The format for National Doubles Finals is:
   1 South v 4 North
   2 North v 3 South
   3 North v 2 South
   4 South v 1 North

Rules for Junior events

1. Competitors must be under the appropriate age on the day of the Tournament.

2. Entries will be taken up to and on the day of the Tournament.

3. Competitors may enter events in their own age group and the one immediately above.

4. The number of sets to be played in each event will be at the discretion of the Tournament Organiser.

5. The different events are:
   — u12 Unisex Doubles
   — u14 Mixed Doubles
   — u16 Boy's Doubles
   — u16 Girl's Doubles
   — u18 Mixed Doubles

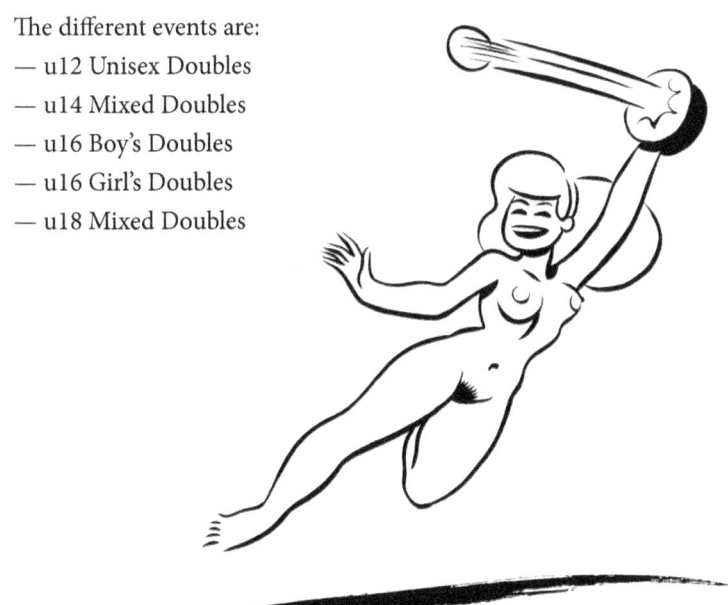

Rules of Eligibility

1. The Senior Section is for players of all ages.

2. The Youth Section is for players under 21 years of age.

3. For the purposes of the AMinA the Youth Section of a Club is regarded as being separate from the Parent Club and must be affiliated to the AMinA in its own right.

4. Juniors are players under 18 years of age.

5. Veterans: Ladies 45 years and over and Gentlemen 50 years and over

6. Junior events and Senior events are separate competitions.

7. Players under 18 years of age may play in the appropriate Junior events (see Appendix III) and in the Senior events representing either the Youth Section or the Senior Section of the Parent Club.

    i.e., They may enter the appropriate Junior events and the may represent either the Youth Section or the Senior Section of the Parent Club in the Mixed Doubles and Men's or Ladies Doubles.

8. Players under 21 years of age may not represent the Youth Section and the Senior Section of the Parent Club in the same competition. i.e., They may not represent the Youth Section in the Mixed Doubles and the Senior Section in the Men's or Ladies Doubles in the same competition.

9. Each club that is affiliated to the AMinA is allowed to send two entries for each event in the Regional qualifying tournaments (providing the above criteria have been satisfied). i.e., A Club can send two Senior teams and two Youth teams to play in the Men's Doubles events, the Ladies Doubles events and the Mixed Doubles events.

ALSO AVAILABLE

Naked as Nature Intended
The Epic Tale of a Nudist Picture by Pamela Green
with photographs by Douglas "Dambuster" Webb DFM

The Naked Truth About Harrison Marks
The notorious biography by Franklyn Wood

Amazons of Yesteryear.
An action packed and rare collection of
wrestling women of the 1940s and '50s

Naked in the Menagerie
A playful look at Eve accompanied by her animal friends

Nudist Camp Follies
An intimate look at the natural and free
atmosphere in Sun Clubs

Nymphs and Naiads
Beauty unadorned and outdoors

Poise and Pose
A magnificent series of photographs of female beauty
taken in the studio

Order on line at wolfbait.co.uk

www.ingramcontent.com/pod-product-compliance
Lightning Source LLC
Chambersburg PA
CBHW060543080526
44586CB00012B/845